W9-BQV-698

THE **MAKING** OF THE **MODERN WORLD**

1945 TO THE PRESENT

Governance and the Quest for Security

BOOKS IN THE SERIES

Culture and Customs in a Connected World

Education, Poverty, and Inequality

Food, Population, and the Environment

Governance and the Quest for Security

Health and Medicine

Migration and Refugees

Science and Technology

Trade, Economic Life, and Globalization

Women, Minorities, and Changing Social Structures

THE **MAKING** OF THE **MODERN WORLD**

1945 TO THE PRESENT

Governance and the Quest for Security

AUTHOR AND SERIES ADVISOR

Ruud van Dijk

Mason Crest

Mason Crest
450 Parkway Drive, Suite D
Broomall, PA 19008
www.masoncrest.com

Produced and developed by MTM Publishing.
www.mtmpublishing.com

President and Project Coordinator: Valerie Tomaselli
Designer: Sherry Williams, Oxygen Design Group
Copyeditor: Lee Motteler, GeoMap Corp.
Editorial Coordinator: Andrea St. Aubin
Proofreader: Peter Jaskowiak

ISBN: 978-1-4222-3638-3
Series ISBN: 978-1-4222-3634-5
Ebook ISBN: 978-1-4222-8282-3

Library of Congress Cataloging-in-Publication Data
On file

Printed and bound in the United States of America.

First printing
9 8 7 6 5 4 3 2 1

QR CODES AND LINKS TO THIRD PARTY CONTENT
You may gain access to certain third party content ("Third Party Sites") by scanning and using the QR Codes that appear in this publication (the "QR Codes"). We do not operate or control in any respect any information, products or services on such Third Party Sites linked to by us via the QR Codes included in this publication, and we assume no responsibility for any materials you may access using the QR Codes. Your use of the QR Codes may be subject to terms, limitations, or restrictions set forth in the applicable terms of use or otherwise established by the owners of the Third Party Sites. Our linking to such Third Party Sites via the QR Codes does not imply an endorsement or sponsorship of such Third Party Sites, or the information, products or services offered on or through the Third Party Sites, nor does it imply an endorsement or sponsorship of this publication by the owners of such Third Party Sites.

Contents

Series Introduction 6

CHAPTER 1: From War to Cold War 9

CHAPTER 2: The "High Cold War," 1947–1962. .17

CHAPTER 3: Globalization's Challenge to the Cold War Order, 1963–1988 31

CHAPTER 4: The World Order Challenged, 1990–2015 45

Timeline 54

Further Research. 59

Index. 60

Photo Credits 63

About the Author and Advisor 64

KEY ICONS TO LOOK FOR:

Words to understand: These words with their easy-to-understand definitions will increase the reader's understanding of the text while building vocabulary skills.

Sidebars: This boxed material within the main text allows readers to build knowledge, gain insights, explore possibilities, and broaden their perspectives by weaving together additional information to provide realistic and holistic perspectives.

Educational Videos: Readers can view videos by scanning our QR codes, providing them with additional educational content to supplement the text. Examples include news coverage, moments in history, speeches, iconic sports moments and much more!

Text-dependent questions: These questions send the reader back to the text for more careful attention to the evidence presented there.

Research projects: Readers are pointed toward areas of further inquiry connected to each chapter. Suggestions are provided for projects that encourage deeper research and analysis.

Series Introduction

In 1945, at the end of World War II, the world had to start afresh in many ways. The war had affected the entire world, destroying cities, sometimes entire regions, and killing millions. At the end of the war, millions more were displaced or on the move, while hunger, disease, and poverty threatened survivors everywhere the war had been fought.

Politically, the old, European-dominated order had been discredited. Western European democracies had failed to stop Hitler, and in Asia they had been powerless against imperial Japan. The autocratic, militaristic Axis powers had been defeated. But their victory was achieved primarily through the efforts of the Soviet Union—a communist dictatorship—and the United States, which was the only democracy powerful enough to aid Great Britain and the other Allied powers in defeating the Axis onslaught. With the European colonial powers weakened, the populations of their respective empires now demanded their independence.

The war had truly been a global catastrophe. It underlined the extent to which peoples and countries around the world were interconnected and interdependent. However, the search for shared approaches to major, global challenges in the postwar world—symbolized by the founding of the United Nations—was soon overshadowed by the Cold War. The leading powers in this contest, the United States and the Soviet Union, represented mutually exclusive visions for the postwar world. The Soviet Union advocated collectivism, centrally planned economies, and a leading role for the Communist Party. The United States sought to promote liberal democracy, symbolized by free markets and open political systems. Each believed fervently in the promise and justice of its vision for the future. And neither thought it could compromise on what it considered vital interests. Both were concerned about whose influence would dominate Europe, for example, and to whom newly independent nations in the non-Western world would pledge their allegiance. As a result, the postwar world would be far from peaceful.

As the Cold War proceeded, peoples living beyond the Western world and outside the control of the Soviet Union began to find their voices. Driven by decolonization, the developing world, or so-called Third World, took on a new importance. In particular, countries in these areas were potential allies on both sides of the Cold War. As the newly independent peoples established their own identities and built viable states, they resisted the sometimes coercive pull of the Cold War superpowers, while also trying to use them for their own ends. In addition, a new Communist China, established in 1949 and the largest country in the developing world, was deeply entangled within the Cold War contest between communist and capitalist camps. Over the coming decades, however, it would come to act ever more independently from either the United States or the Soviet Union.

During the war, governments had made significant strides in developing new technologies in areas such as aviation, radar, missile technology, and, most ominous, nuclear energy. Scientific and technological breakthroughs achieved in a military context held promise for civilian applications, and thus were poised to contribute to recovery and, ultimately, prosperity. In other fields, it also seemed time for a fresh start. For example, education could be used to "re-educate" members of aggressor nations and further Cold War agendas, but education could also help more people take advantage of, and contribute to, the possibilities of the new age of science and technology.

For several decades after 1945, the Cold War competition seemed to dominate, and indeed define, the postwar world. Driven by ideology, the conflict extended into politics, economics, science and technology, and culture. Geographically, it came to affect virtually the entire world. From our twenty-first-century vantage point, however, it is clear that well before the Cold War's end in the late 1980s, the world had been moving on from the East-West conflict.

Looking back, it appears that, despite divisions—between communist and capitalist camps, or between developed and developing countries—the world after 1945 was growing more and more interconnected. After the Cold War, this increasingly came to be called "globalization." People in many different places faced shared challenges. And as time went on, an awareness of this interconnectedness grew. One response by people in and outside of governments was to seek common approaches, to think and act globally. Another was to protect national, local, or private autonomy, to keep the outside world at bay. Neither usually existed by itself; reality was generally some combination of the two.

Thematically organized, the nine volumes in this series explore how the post–World War II world gradually evolved from the fractured ruins of 1945, through the various crises of the Cold War and the decolonization process, to a world characterized by interconnectedness and interdependence. The accounts in these volumes reinforce each other, and are best studied together. Taking them as a whole will build a broad understanding of the ways in which "globalization" has become the defining feature of the world in the early twenty-first century.

However, the volumes are designed to stand on their own. Tracing the evolution of trade and the global economy, for example, the reader will learn enough about the political context to get a broader understanding of the times. Of course, studying economic developments will likely lead to curiosity about scientific and technological progress, social and cultural change, poverty and education, and more. In other words, studying one volume should lead to interest in the others. In the end, no element of our globalizing world can be fully understood in isolation.

The volumes do not have to be read in a specific order. It is best to be led by one's own interests in deciding where to start. What we recommend is a curious, critical stance throughout the study of the world's history since World War II: to keep asking questions about the causes of events, to keep looking for connections to deepen your understanding of how we have gotten to where we are today. If students achieve this goal with the help of our volumes, we—and they—will have succeeded.

—Ruud van Dijk

WORDS TO UNDERSTAND

ideology: set of ideas, concepts, and values forming the basis of a society, culture, or nation.

interventionists: those who believe that being engaged in the affairs of other countries is the best policy.

isolationists: those who believe that staying removed from the affairs of other countries is the best policy.

pragmatist: someone who believes in a practical, realistic approach to making decisions and solving problems.

ABOVE: German leader Adolf Hitler during a parade in June 1940 in Munich, Germany, celebrating early Nazi victories in World War II, with his ally, Italian leader Benito Mussolini.

1

From War to Cold War

On February 17, 1941, the publisher Henry R. Luce intervened in the passionate debate in the United States between **isolationists** and **interventionists** with an article in *Life* magazine, entitled "The American Century." With Hitler on the march in Europe and Japan attacking its East Asian neighbors, freedom and democracy, according to Luce, were in mortal danger, not just across the world, but in America as well. It was high time and in the United States' interest, he wrote, that the country take up a leadership role.

The "world crisis" of 1941 posed real dangers, and Luce sought to paint an optimistic picture of what the United States could contribute to peace and stability while promoting "American principles" around the world. Luce would turn out to be prophetic, because for much of the remaining twentieth century, his country indeed played a leading role in international politics. In fact, during the 1990s the French foreign minister referred to the United States as a "hyperpower." To an extent not matched even by the British Empire it replaced as a global leader, the United States shaped the international order of the post–World War II era. Because the U.S.-led order, unlike its communist alternative, also survived the Cold War, the influence of the United States on global governance in the current era of globalization remains paramount. The twentieth century, Luce argued, must be the American Century.

A Central Role for the United States

That the United States came to play this role had more to do with the vision and political skill of its president at the time of the Second World War, Franklin D. Roosevelt, than with Luce's influence. Perhaps even more important was America's economic power, which far exceeded that of any other power in the world. Still, by the time Luce published his article, the president was busy trying to convince the American public of how American prosperity, and ultimately also American freedoms, depended on freedom and democracy elsewhere.

Henry Luce, with his wife, Claire Booth Luce.

This was part of Luce's message, too. It was based on lessons he, Roosevelt, and others of their generation had drawn from the years after World War I, when the United States, in the words of one historian, had stuck to a policy of "involvement without commitment" with the problems of the world. This time around, Roosevelt believed, the United States not only should play a part in the defeat of Hitler's Germany and the containment of imperial Japan, it should also lead the postwar world to ensure that American principles thrived everywhere.

Even before the formal entry of the United States, Roosevelt had formulated general war aims. In August of 1941, together with British prime minister Winston Churchill, Roosevelt issued the Atlantic Charter, a set of principles envisioning a liberal-democratic postwar world—one in which free trade and self-government were the norms. In the interest of allied cooperation against the aggressor states, certain concerns, such as the future of the European colonial empires, were kept deliberately vague.

By that time, Great Britain and the United States were also supporting the Soviet Union against Hitler's Germany, which had attacked it in June. In spite of the fact that he had turned his country into a brutal communist dictatorship (and originally, in 1939, made common cause with Hitler), Soviet leader Joseph Stalin declared himself in support of the Atlantic Charter, thus giving Roosevelt hope that cooperation would continue after the war. As the war turned to the Allies' favor after 1942, discussions over the makeup of the postwar world became more important. With the looming defeat of Germany and Japan and the weakening of the European powers as a result of two world wars, the United States and the Soviet Union would likely decide whether a peaceful and stable world would emerge.

Divisions between Allies Emerge

Already during the war, significant differences between the two sides were evident, even though in 1944 Stalin

Leaders of the major Allied forces during World War II—Soviet premiere Joseph Stalin, U.S. president Franklin Roosevelt, and British prime minister Winston Churchill (seated, left to right)—meeting for a conference in Tehran, Iran, in 1943.

THE UNITED NATIONS

The League of Nations was established after World War I as a shared forum for nations to cooperate on shared challenges. However, the League had proved unable to play that part effectively in the 1920s and 1930s, in part because the United States did not join it.

After World War II, the founders of the UN sought a balance between internationalism, where nations subordinate their own interests to those shared by all; national sovereignty, which guards the independence of individual nations; and the special role played by the great powers. The UN's Security Council would be the organ to pass resolutions binding for all nations, but it could only do so if none of the five permanent members—the United States, the Soviet Union, China, Great Britain, and France—used its veto power. In the contentious world of the Cold War, this meant that the UN would often be at the sidelines in international disputes.

agreed to let the Soviet Union join the new United Nations organization. He declined participation in the financial-economic bodies (the International Monetary Fund and the World Bank) organized at the Bretton Woods Conference of the same year. More than the UN, Bretton Woods represented America's vision for a new world order along liberal-democratic lines, with market economies and open societies. Stalin's vision was close to the opposite.

Ideology drove the two sides apart after 1945, despite the potential benefits of cooperation. Just as U.S. leaders believed liberal democracy was destined to spread to more and more countries, Stalin believed that history was inevitably moving in the direction of a communist world. Not only that, he believed that the alternative—capitalism—was relentlessly hostile to the Soviet Union and its allies. Communist-capitalist relations were a zero-sum struggle for power and ultimately survival, he was convinced, with no coming out ahead: a gain for one side automatically meant a setback for the other, and the two sides could not permanently coexist peacefully.

Stalin was also a **pragmatist**, however. He understood that the Soviet Union was weaker and needed time to recover from the war; in 1945 he was not looking for a new one. Instead, he hoped to continue the cooperation begun during the war—without jeopardizing any vital Soviet interests, such as control of Eastern Europe or influence in postwar Germany. This proved to be impossible: the 1945–1947 period showed that differences between East and West, soon known as the Cold War, were not based on misunderstandings but instead stemmed from mutually exclusive visions for the postwar world.

Where Stalin was convinced of irreconcilable enmity, American leaders took almost two years to come to the same conclusion—and that Stalin would not follow the American lead. Already early in 1945, during the war, Stalin charted his own course in occupying Poland, where he imposed communist rule. Of course, that summer Roosevelt's successor, Harry S. Truman, casually told the Soviet leader of the successful test of an atomic weapon, the result of a top-secret program Washington had pursued with Britain during the war without informing the Soviet Union. The U.S. military, seeking a speedy end to the war in the Pacific, next made its own decisions in using the other two available bombs against the Japanese cities of Hiroshima and Nagasaki.

U.S. president Harry S. Truman (on left) followed by Soviet premiere Joseph Stalin at the Potsdam Conference on August 1, 1945. During the meeting, Truman casually told Stalin about the U.S. testing of an atomic weapon, which the United States used on Japan just one week later.

Following the dropping of the bombs on Japan, the two sides, under a UN umbrella, explored possibilities for the international control of atomic energy for several months, but suspicions on both sides ran too deep for this ever to succeed. At the first report of the damage in Hiroshima and Nagasaki, Stalin ordered an all-out effort to build a Soviet nuclear weapon to break the United States' atomic monopoly, and it was highly unlikely that the United States would voluntarily yield its lead in the arms race. With regard to the future of Germany, jointly occupied at the end of the war, the standoff continued. East and West agreed to disagree, thereby laying the foundation for the founding, in 1949, of two separate German states, one allied with the West and the other with the Soviet Union.

Containment and the Two-Camps Theory

The year 1946 saw crises over Iran and Turkey, both instances where Stalin appeared to be probing weak areas on the Soviet Union's periphery. In both cases, the United States led the international opposition. Publicly, Stalin warned the Soviet people that capitalism would continue to produce new wars, and former British prime minister Churchill spoke of an "Iron Curtain" having been lowered through the center of Europe.

Writing from the embassy in Moscow, the American diplomat and Russian expert George F. Kennan warned his government that, given Soviet ideology, it was an illusion to think that genuine cooperation was possible with Moscow. Instead, the United States had to accept that for Stalin, the Soviet Union could only be secure if the West was weak, its influence undermined all around the world, and that the Soviet Union would try to make it so. Instead of one new world order, the postwar world was in the process of being divided in two.

Formal "declarations of Cold War" followed in 1947. On March 12, President Truman told a joint session of Congress, "It must be the policy of the United States to support free peoples who are resisting subjugation by armed minorities or by outside pressure." These words were at the core of what became known as the "Truman Doctrine": a foreign policy aiming to "contain" the further advance of communism and Soviet power.

Truman's government was reacting to the British withdrawal from a civil war in Greece, where leftist, communist-supported forces appeared to be winning. While the Greek Civil War ultimately resolved in Washington's favor, the United States also worried about slow economic recovery in Western Europe. Lack of economic progress there might enhance the influence of local communist parties, especially in France and Italy, taking orders from Moscow. If the United States did not step into the breach, Stalin's influence in Europe, as well as the Middle East, might increase. It might grow so much that the balance of power in these areas, so vital to U.S. national interests, would shift decisively in Moscow's favor.

The civil war in Greece was rooted in divisions created during the occupation of the country by Nazi Germany and Italy during World War II. Shown here are members of ELAS (Greek People's Liberation Army), a communist-leaning guerilla group fighting against the occupation.

"Containment" was an alternative to a new war, on the one hand, and not acting against Soviet expansion, on the other. It was a strategy to defend U.S. interests around the world and ultimately to promote a liberal-democratic international order. Even though the advocates of containment publicly sounded the alarm in making the case for it, they did not believe that military force was the only way to carry it out.

Aside from funding made available for the Greek and Turkish governments, the first implementation of "containment" was the Marshall Plan, a large economic aid package for the countries of Western Europe. U.S. planners such as Kennan believed that when Europeans regained their faith in the viability of market economies and democratic politics, communism would lose most if not all of its appeal. In response to the Truman Doctrine, the Soviet government proclaimed its "two camps" theory: on one side the U.S.-led "imperialist" countries, preparing a new war, and on the other the Soviet Union–led peace-loving "anti-fascist" countries. If you were not with these "peace-loving forces," you were an enemy. The Cold War was now formally on.

Text-Dependent Questions

1. What was the Atlantic Charter and when was it signed?

2. Define "containment" and the "two-camps" theory.

3. What were some of the key issues that divided the United States and the Soviet Union between 1945 and 1947?

Research Projects

1. Using your library's resources and reliable Internet sources, write a short history of the Manhattan Project to build an atomic bomb. Why is the Manhattan Project relevant for a discussion of the origins of the Cold War?

2. Research the civil war in Greece, the one that worried U.S. policy makers so much in 1947. Prepare a class presentation, answering the following questions: What were its origins? What were the two sides fighting for? Why did it matter to the United States what kind of government Greece had?

Educational Videos

Potsdam Conference: Big Three: Truman, Stalin & Churchill Meet in Berlin 1945 US OWI Newsreel
Page 12
Film footage of President Truman's travels to the Potsdam Conference; includes a speech by Truman to U.S. troops in occupied Germany.
Published on YouTube by Jeff Quitney, Improved Documentary and Training Films.
https://www.youtube.com/watch?v=KdTmrusxCag&feature=youtu.be

Street Fighting in Athens (1945)
Page 13–14
Newsreel of the fighting in Athens during the Greek Civil War, produced by the British newsreel and documentary broadcaster, British Pathé.
Published on YouTube by British Pathé.
https://www.youtube.com/watch?v=KZ8iNDBaGuA

ABOVE: The construction of a flotation plant to be used for the mining of sulfur, which was undertaken in Sicily, a province of Italy, with money from the Marshall Fund.

WORDS TO UNDERSTAND

blockade: barrier built not to be passable.

coup d'état: forceful removal of a political leader.

credibility: capacity to inspire confidence and belief.

dysfunctional: broken and incapable of operating correctly.

nationalist: relating to loyalty and a sense of belonging to a nation.

precipice: steep ledge or cliff.

rearmament: rebuilding the military capacity of a country or other entity.

2

The "High Cold War," 1947–1962

With the Cold War formally on, both sides began to consolidate their respective spheres of influence. They were anticipating the struggle for regions in what would become known as the Third World, nations not yet committed to one side or another. For their part, Third World peoples had agendas of their own, primarily focused on gaining independence from the old European colonial empires. Ultimately, however, most of them could not avoid being drawn into the struggle for influence between the superpowers.

The Cold War Takes Shape and Heats Up

In that struggle, the United States appeared to have the upper hand after 1947. Not only did economic recovery get underway in Western Europe, Washington, together with its allies France and Great Britain, also succeeded in laying the groundwork for a separate West German state. Crucially, West Germans themselves played a central role in this process, and in this they were helped by Stalin. In response to Western steps toward a West German state, the Soviet dictator in 1948 began a **blockade** of the western part of the old German capital, Berlin, which was located in the Soviet zone of occupation but was occupied by the Western allies.

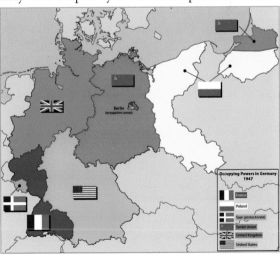

Zones of occupation in Germany following World War II. The areas shaded in pale yellow show the regions Germany lost to Poland and Russia following the war.

The blockade was a crude way to extract concessions from the Western allies, but it backfired. The West organized the famous "Berlin Airlift," which supplied West Berlin with food and other necessities. Also, many West Germans became willing to accept a formal division of their country and began to side with the West in the Cold War, even if this meant that millions of their fellow Germans in the Soviet zone would be condemned to living under Soviet communism. Aiming to close ranks in his part of Europe, but appearing once again to seek expansion, Stalin in early 1948 also ordered a communist **coup d'état** in Czechoslovakia.

These moves by the Soviets led to the founding of a military alliance between the countries of Western Europe and the United States and Canada, the North Atlantic Treaty Organization (NATO), another setback for Stalin. So in the spring of 1949, containment appeared to be working: Stalin was being locked out of Western Europe, including the most populous and wealthy part of Germany; communism as an alternative to capitalism was losing its appeal; and the United States, through NATO, had committed itself to the defense of its European allies. In Asia, meanwhile, it was the United States alone that was determining the pace and direction of Japan's rehabilitation.

This U.S. transport plane—loaded with sacks of flour—is ready to take off from the Rhine Main Airfield for the Templehof Air Base in West Berlin during the Berlin Airlift in July 1948.

The Communist New Fourth Army in January 1946 during a ceasefire in the Chinese civil war between communist and nationalist forces.

Then, in a matter of weeks, everything changed. First, in August, came the news that the Soviet Union had successfully tested an atomic bomb. This was much sooner than anybody, certainly the American public, had been led to expect. Then, on October 1, 1949, Chinese communist leader Mao Zedong proclaimed the founding of the People's Republic of China, confirming the communist victory in China's long civil war over the nationalists, long supported by the United States. The most populous country in the world was now under a communist government.

An empire going back many centuries, China was weakened in the nineteenth century through internal divisions and incursions from Western powers. After the revolution of 1911, a **nationalist** government came to power, but it was challenged in the 1920s by a burgeoning communist movement. Armed struggle began in 1927, but in the 1930s the civil war was mostly suspended due to the Japanese invasion of the country. After the end of World War II in 1945, fighting resumed, with the United States trying to mediate while also supporting the government run by the nationalists. The communist victory in 1949, therefore, was also a defeat for the United States.

U.S. domestic politics were never the same. The Soviet Union and its allies appeared to have changed the

THE "THIRD WORLD"

First used in French in the early 1950s, the term "Third World" was used broadly during the Cold War to refer to the non-Western developing world. "Third World" echoes the "third estate" of the era before the French Revolution of 1789: the most populous but least represented part of the population, and this became one of the term's meanings after 1945.

During the Cold War, "Third World" indicated those countries that refused to be ruled by either one of the rival superpowers and their ideologies. For developing nations, many of which had only recently gained independence from the old European colonial powers, the Cold War was not their quest, and they looked for alternative models, a "third way." Later, the term "Global South" was also used, as most Third World countries could be found in the Southern Hemisphere.

The UN was an initiative by elites from the traditional, great Western powers—the "Global North." Some envisioned the organization as a tool to preserve Western dominance, in spite of decolonization. However, led by India's prime minister Jawaharlal Nehru, newly independent nations demanded that their rights and those of peoples remaining under colonial rule be taken seriously. Through their growing numbers in the UN General Assembly, they were able to make their mark as independent nations. The paradoxical outcome was that national sovereignty, along with a growing division between the global "North" and "South," came to characterize the internationalist UN more than many had expected in 1945.

momentum in the Cold War. And these setbacks for the United States and the West had consequences for the strategy of containment. First, it became militarized. In January 1950, President Truman approved the development of a new type of nuclear weapon, the hydrogen bomb, thus putting the nuclear arms race in a higher gear; later in the year he also approved a tripling of the defense budget.

The budget increase came after the North Korean invasion of South Korea in June, which turned the Cold War hot. The United States came to the defense of the South; Communist China intervened to help the North; and the Soviet Union supported both its communist allies, China and North Korea. The war did not escalate beyond Korea, but it seemed clear that Moscow and its allies were on the offensive in Asia. This led to a second major change in containment and, indeed, the Cold War as a whole: it now focused more and more on the Third World.

Competing for the Third World

Major changes had been afoot in the Third World, especially in East Asia following the defeat of Japan in 1945. Encouraged by the weakening of European colonial powers such as Great Britain, France, and the Netherlands, Indians, Pakistanis, Vietnamese, Indonesians, and others proclaimed their independence. In the case of the Indian subcontinent, the British colonizer accepted the end of its rule. The French and Dutch, however, insisted on continued ties, even though they said they were in favor of more local autonomy. The result in both Indochina and Indonesia was colonial wars, both initially related only weakly to the emerging Cold War.

For the United States, the stakes were high: on the one hand, the French especially were crucial allies in Europe; on the other hand, the United States understood that colonial empires were finished, and it wanted to be on the right side of history. The problem, as the Americans saw it, was the leading role communists played in many Third World struggles for independence, especially Indochina. In Indonesia, the leader of the independence struggle, Sukarno, was an anticommunist. Consequently, the United States in 1949 leaned on its Dutch ally to stop its resistance to Indonesian independence, but in Indochina, where the communist Ho Chi Minh led the fight, things were less straightforward.

While Indochina's independence struggle was complex, the way it drew along Cold War dividing lines was clear. In early 1950, as a result of Mao's victory in China, Ho gained a powerful ally right across the border from North Vietnam. Prior to 1949, the United States had mostly been on the fence in regard to France's war in Indochina; in 1950 it felt it could not risk a French defeat and see another Asian country fall to communist rule. The United States began to support the French war effort, marking the beginning of an involvement that would climax in the big American war in Vietnam in the late 1960s and early 1970s. And so, through the actions of great powers on both sides, the struggle in Indochina got drawn into the Cold War. There were many other Third World struggles to follow.

A 1921 photo of Nguyen Ai Quoc, later known as Ho Chi Minh, when he was an Indochinese delegate to the French Communist Congress in Marseilles, France.

Western European Resurgence

In spite of, or maybe thanks to, the developments in Asia, the consolidation of the American-promoted liberal-democratic order in Europe continued in the 1950s, increasingly through initiatives from the Europeans themselves. The Soviet Union, meanwhile, struggled to create any allegiance or prosperity in its part of Europe.

In the first half of the decade, the rehabilitation of West Germany continued when, following an initiative by French foreign minister Robert Schuman, the countries of Western Europe created a European Coal and Steel Community (ECSC). Established in 1952, the ECSC would be the basis for the European Economic Community after 1957, and for today's European Union. The United States and the Europeans also collaborated with the West German government led by Konrad Adenauer on West German **rearmament**. In 1955 this led to West German membership in NATO. In less than ten years, the Cold War, the success of West Germany's democracy, and the country's economic revival had turned the Germans from defeated foes into key members of the Western alliance and the budding European community of nations.

The Soviet Union was powerless to interfere with these developments, although through various political initiatives it tried. Moscow's **credibility**, however, was low. In part this stemmed from the repressive policies it imposed on its own people and those of the communist-led countries of Eastern Europe. Economically, the Soviet Union had much less to offer than the United States. This was due to the inefficiencies of its top-down command economy, which regulated everything from the country's overall economic policy to the kinds of products individual firms would produce. It was also the result of the devastation from World War II. On top of all this, Soviet politics had become **dysfunctional** as Stalin aged and became ever more paranoid. The dictator died in March 1953, leading to a transition period in the Kremlin that lasted until about 1956. At that time, Nikita Khrushchev emerged as the new leader.

In the interim, Stalin's successors were engaged in an internal struggle for power, and they also had to contain the political-economic crisis in Eastern Europe that had emerged during Stalin's final years. In June 1953, it was Soviet tanks that saved the communist regime of East Germany (the German Democratic Republic, or GDR) against a popular uprising. In 1956, Moscow also intervened militarily in Hungary to defend communist power. The best the Soviet Union was able to do in Europe in the 1950s was try to defend what it had gained after the war. Hence, for example, in 1955 the Warsaw Pact Treaty Organization was founded as Moscow's answer to NATO. The building of a wall between East and West Berlin followed in 1961. Many educated East German citizens left for a more prosperous and free life in West Germany through Berlin, and communist leaders feared that this "brain drain" threatened the survival of the state.

The member states of the European Coal and Steel Community (ECSC), which later became the basis for the European Economic Community and eventually the European Union. The founding members are in darker green.

U.S. president John F. Kennedy, on the platform in front, second from right, in June 1963 along the Berlin Wall at Checkpoint Charlie, one of the most well-known crossings between East and West Berlin, when he delivered his famous line "Ich bin ein Berliner" ("I am a Berliner").

President Truman with Prime Minister Mohammad Mossadegh of Iran in October 1951; prior to visiting the president, Mossadegh spoke at the UN to defend Iran's takeover of the country's oil industry. Just two years later, after President Eisenhower took office, the CIA helped to implement his overthrow.

Trends in Europe did little to reassure the United States. Most of its politicians chose to emphasize the danger posed by communism at home and abroad. Policy was often based on a worst-case scenario for Soviet behavior. After the "loss" of China to communism and the end of the U.S. monopoly on atomic weapons in 1949, Republican members of Congress and others intensified the so-called Red Scare—a hunt for communist sympathizers, especially in the government. This would limit the room for alternative views or policies in the United States.

Intervening in the Third World

With regard to the Third World, the assumption was that the Soviet Union and China would seek to take over more and more countries so that eventually the global balance of power would favor communism. In practice, this meant that Washington, like its adversaries in Moscow and Beijing, viewed Third World struggles for independence through a Cold War lens: communist-led wars for independence were less about independence than about spreading communism.

Independent nationalist governments in Third World countries, meanwhile, especially in countries traditionally under Western influence such as Iran and Guatemala, could not be trusted. Instead, the assumption of the new administration led by Republican Dwight D. Eisenhower was that Third World nationalists either already sympathized with Moscow or would do so in the future. In 1953, Eisenhower directed the Central Intelligence Agency (CIA) to help overthrow the Mossadegh government in Iran; in 1954 the CIA got the same assignment with regard to the Arbenz government in Guatemala. Most ominously, when in 1954 the forces of Ho Chi Minh defeated the French in Indochina, the Eisenhower administration stepped in to prevent Ho's communist government from taking over all of Vietnam. The country was divided between North and South, with the United States as the major backer of a noncommunist South Vietnam.

As the struggle for the Third World intensified, Washington also tried to help newly independent countries with development assistance, but anticommunism often got in the way. What to Americans appeared to be a prudent approach seemed like the actions of old European colonial powers in the eyes of Third World peoples. To the Soviet Union and China, meanwhile, U.S. interventions in Third World countries only confirmed that East and West were engaged in a zero-sum struggle for world supremacy.

THE GENEVA CONFERENCE OF 1954 AND VIETNAM

Planned in early 1954 by Western and communist powers to discuss issues surrounding Korea, the Geneva Conference, when it got underway in April, soon was dominated by developments in Indochina. On May 7, the communist-led independence movement in Vietnam, the Vietminh, decisively defeated the French colonial armies at Dien Bien Phu.

Rather than accept the Vietminh's victory, the United States put pressure on its French ally to stay in Vietnam and insisted that the southern part of Vietnam stay out of communist hands. Pressured by the Soviet Union and China, the Vietminh agreed and Vietnam was formally divided. National elections, envisioned for 1956, never took place. After 1954, the United States quickly took the place of the French as the main sponsor of South Vietnam. Communist-led North Vietnam would never accept the division of the country.

A Cold War Arms Race

The nuclear arms race, meanwhile, had become an important driver of Cold War competition. By 1955 both the United States and the Soviet Union had successfully tested hydrogen bombs. Such thermonuclear devices could be hundreds of times more powerful than the atomic bombs dropped on Japan. Both sides assumed the worst about each other's intentions, which not only meant larger and larger nuclear arsenals, but also a race to develop new delivery systems, especially rockets.

In 1957, the Soviet Union actually took the lead in this part of the arms race when it launched Sputnik, the first satellite to be put into orbit. In 1961, the Soviets still appeared to be ahead when they put the first human being into orbit and returned him safely to earth. Americans felt vulnerable to a surprise attack, and they wondered if the Soviet Union and its allies might indeed be getting the upper hand. In reality, the United States was never far behind, and after 1957 it quickly caught up and then surpassed the Soviet Union in missile technology and construction. But Cold War anxieties among the public and in Congress in the late 1950s and early 1960s once again limited U.S. policy options, while the lack of meaningful East-West diplomacy added to tensions.

Crisis in Cuba

Thrown into this dangerous mix in 1959 was an anti-American revolution on the island of Cuba, led by Fidel Castro. Opposed by Washington, Castro quickly aligned himself with an enthusiastic Khrushchev, who viewed the Cuban revolution as confirmation that the political tide ran with communism in the Third World. The bonds became tighter after a failed CIA-engineered invasion of Cuba by Cuban exiles. Khrushchev wanted to protect his new friend in America's backyard. Convinced that the Soviet Union could not sustain the expensive arms race with the powerful United States, he also hoped to force a truce upon Washington. Once that happened, Soviet communism, he believed, would prove that it was a superior system for delivering prosperity and justice to the greatest number of people.

Pressed to stand up to the Americans by China's leader, Mao, who competed with him for leadership of Third World liberation movements, in 1962 Khrushchev tried to solve all his problems in one fell swoop. The Soviet Union would secretly deploy medium-range nuclear missiles on Cuba, he decided. Once they were in place, Washington would have to leave Castro alone and, just as important, negotiate about the arms race on Soviet terms. The American discovery of the weapons in October, and Washington's demand that they be removed, led to the most dangerous crisis of the Cold War, the Cuban Missile Crisis. Only at the last minute did Khrushchev back down, although President John F. Kennedy also made concessions to resolve the standoff.

Coming to the **precipice** of a nuclear war in October 1962 led Khrushchev and Kennedy to try to defuse the East-West competition. A nuclear war would only have losers, and some scientists argued it could be the end of human life. During the

The first test of a full-scale hydrogen bomb, conducted by the United States in October 1952, over Enewetak, an atoll in the Pacific Ocean, in an operation code-named Ivy Mike.

Cuban Missile Crisis, the two leaders had also discovered that in a high-stakes crisis situation, with large military organizations on high alert during a time of urgency, a rational decision-making process directed by political leaders might take a back seat. In short, the nuclear danger was a shared problem, and it was in the interest of both sides to contain it.

In 1963, the White House and the Kremlin established a direct telephone connection for future crisis management. The same year, joined by Great Britain, they signed the Partial Test Ban Treaty that banned the testing of nuclear weapons in the atmosphere, underwater, or in outer space. These developments did not signify the end of the Cold War by any means, but they nonetheless inaugurated a new era in which international cooperation, also across Cold War dividing lines, became more and more widespread.

This map, showing the range (in NMs, or nautical miles) of nuclear missiles sites being constructed in Cuba, was used in secret meetings in the United States during the Cuban Missile Crisis in 1962.

Text-Dependent Questions

1. How did it appear to Americans that the Soviet Union could be winning the Cold War in the 1950s?

2. What did it mean to the United States to be "on the right side of history" in the Global South? Why did the Soviet Union and Communist China seem to have the advantage here too?

3. How did the Cuban Missile Crisis in 1962 lead U.S. and Soviet leaders to try to defuse the Cold War conflict?

Research Projects

1. Write a short history of the divided city of Berlin from the Berlin Airlift of 1948–1949 until the building of the Berlin Wall in 1961. Why was Berlin such a contested issue at this time?

2. Research the 1959 revolution in Cuba. In particular, why could it be called an "anti-American" revolution? Why is it important to understand the history of United States–Cuban relations prior to 1959 in order to answer this question? Present your findings in a brief report, to discuss with your class.

Educational Video

Kennedy Trip: Irish Roar Welcome after German Visit
Page 23

Film footage of President Kennedy's trip to Berlin in 1963, his speech "Ich bin ein Berliner" ("I am a Berliner") at the Berlin Wall, and his visit to Dublin, Ireland, after. Published online by the John F. Kennedy Presidential Library and Museum.
http://www.jfklibrary.org/Asset-Viewer/8AsPSPwoWUaGYu7IZt-1K4g.aspx.

Test launch of a tethered Minuteman missile at the Air Force Rocket Propulsion Laboratory at Edwards Air Force Base. The Minuteman was a critical component in the U.S. nuclear arsenal during the Cold War and after.

WORDS TO UNDERSTAND

abolitionism: commitment to abolish or reverse a policy.

allegiance: loyalty.

convergence: the process of becoming more uniform.

guerillas: irregular fighters, not belonging to a regular army.

interdependence: being mutually dependent, or reliant, on each other.

nonproliferation: ending the spread of something; here, relating to nuclear weapons.

status quo: conditions as they currently are.

CHAPTER

3

Globalization's Challenge to the Cold War Order, 1963–1988

After the Cuban Missile Crisis, the Cold War continued for more than two decades, and well into the 1980s it was hard to imagine a world not dominated by it. In hindsight, however, it is clear that the Cold War order was under pressure more and more by forces associated today with "globalization." Defined as more intensive and faster connections between people worldwide ("space-time compression") driven by technological innovations (production, communication, mobility) and leading to greater **interdependence** (for example through the emergence of a global economy), globalization was making a comeback by the late 1950s.

Prior to World War I (1914–1918), the world had experienced rapid globalization also, but for several decades after the war, many countries pursued narrow national agendas. However, under the influence of the Cold War, a global conflict if there ever was one, the world became more interconnected again. This went beyond the emergence of a global economy in the U.S.-led Western part of the world. It also included the growing recognition by more and more people of shared challenges that could only be tackled in a meaningful way across national lines.

The danger of nuclear war was one such challenge. Not only did the United States and the Soviet Union negotiate agreements that aimed to curb the nuclear arms race between them. By the mid-1970s, the great majority of the countries of the world had also signed on to the Nuclear Non-Proliferation Treaty, completed in 1968. Under this treaty, states without nuclear weapons pledged not to seek them and only use nuclear energy for peaceful purposes. Countries already possessing nuclear weapons pledged to work toward ever smaller stockpiles of weapons, with zero across the world as the end goal. Compliance would be monitored by a shared, international institution: the International Atomic Energy Agency.

AN EARLY PERIOD OF GLOBALIZATION

In the decades before World War I started in 1914, the world quickly became a smaller place. Driven by new technologies such as steamships, railroads, and the telegraph, people all over the world could come into contact with each other much more easily and quickly than ever before. Increased world trade, migration, and a certain amount of cultural **convergence** were the result.

Thanks to their control of new technologies, Western countries led the way. Following the example of Britain and its empire, countries such as Germany, the United States, and Japan consolidated their own territories and joined the international competition for power and wealth. Globalization of the late nineteenth century was also the time when many independent non-Western areas were incorporated into existing colonial empires. Increasingly, Western powers competed rather than cooperated with each other. An arms race became part of this era of globalization, which in 1914 ended in the first global war in history.

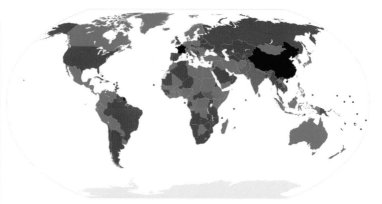

The members of the Nuclear Non-Proliferation Treaty. Countries in blue are members that have nuclear weapons; in green, members *without* nuclear capability. The countries in red—India, Israel, and Pakistan—are not members but are nuclear-capable. North Korea (in yellow), a nuclear power, withdrew in 2003.

Another example of how the world became smaller and more integrated is the organized rise of the Third World, or the Global South, at the time also called the "developing world." These were non-Western countries, especially in Asia, Africa, and the Middle East. Many had been part of European colonial empires, or they were in the process of gaining their independence. Achieving true independence in a world dominated by the Cold War was difficult, and so was finding a way to good governance and prosperity in regions rife with conflict, economic hardship, and fragile government institutions.

Already in 1955, developing countries had gathered in Bandung, Indonesia, to assert their independence from the Cold War rivalries. In 1961 this initiative led to the founding of the Non-Aligned Movement. It can be seen as the first of several attempts by developing nations not only

Official portrait of Indonesia's President Sukarno, who was one of the founders of the Non-Aligned Movement in 1961.

to seek independence and mutual cooperation, but also to remind the industrialized "North" of its responsibility for and interest in fair and full participation of the Third World in the emerging global economy.

In 1964, another landmark in this regard occurred with the first meeting of the United Nations Conference on Trade and Development (UNCTAD). The same year, developing countries also established the "Group of 77" as a way of unifying their voices within the United Nations. Gradually, "development" became a shared goal of North and South. As a result of these initiatives—but also under the influence of television images (new in the 1960s) of war, famine, and general hardship in Third World countries—people in the West became convinced that their countries indeed had a responsibility toward developing countries. "Development," one could say, became a "global norm," just like nuclear **nonproliferation**.

The emergence of "global norms" concerning development issues did not mean that solutions to such issues followed quickly. On the contrary, defining shared global challenges usually only signaled the beginning of fierce political debates over how best to deal with them. Progress, therefore, was generally uneven and far from guaranteed. (For an example in our own time, think of international discussions about what to do about climate change.)

Part of the problem was that the Cold War continued to divide the world, making it difficult for shared organizations such as the United Nations to operate effectively. Decolonization and concerns about the alignment of newly independent countries continued to fuel the East-West conflict. With the dividing lines in Europe fixed in place, both sides believed the Cold War might well be decided in the Third World. There also was the growing divergence between the two leading communist powers: China and the Soviet Union. The so-called Sino-Soviet split led to competition between the two countries for the **allegiance** of independence movements and newly independent nations in the Third World. All this led to complex challenges for Third World movements and governments, but it also offered them opportunities; for example, great power suitors could be played off against each other.

THE BIAFRA CRISIS OF 1969 AND THE RISE OF GLOBAL HUMANITARIANISM

Also known as the Nigerian civil war, the Biafra crisis, especially the famine it produced, was one of the first humanitarian crises gaining worldwide publicity thanks to the relatively new technology of television. Nigeria gained independence from Britain in 1960. Ethnic, political, and economic divisions perpetuated by the British contributed to political strife and violence in the new nation.

In 1967, the Igbo people of the oil-rich southeast declared the Independent Republic of Biafra. War followed, causing much suffering among the population. Efforts by the outside world to provide humanitarian assistance were driven by nongovernmental organizations (NGOs) such as the Red Cross, but also a new group that in 1971 became Doctors Without Borders. The Biafra crisis was among the first humanitarian crises where NGOs, rather than governments, led the world's response.

Center Stage in Vietnam

Communist North Vietnam became particularly skilled at not choosing sides in the Sino-Soviet row. Throughout the 1960s it continued to receive help from both the Soviets and Chinese in its struggle against South Vietnam and its American ally. War had returned to Vietnam around 1960, when communist-led resistance against the South Vietnamese government gave way to a civil war.

The Sino-Soviet competition aside, Vietnam remained a focus of the Cold War. The more the communists were winning, the more involved the United States became in the fighting. In 1964, the Johnson administration decided to Americanize the war. As North Vietnam worked to unify the county under its leadership, the United States bombed it almost continuously, while in the South, American troops assumed most of the fight against the communist **guerillas**.

President Lyndon B. Johnson and his advisers had grave doubts about the chances for success, but they believed the credibility of the United States was at stake. Their country had committed itself to the independence of South Vietnam, and if the United States abandoned South Vietnam, America's allies elsewhere might come to doubt Washington's reliability. Moreover, other countries in Southeast Asia could fall to communism. Finally, Johnson and his advisers feared that the Soviet and Chinese governments could become bolder in other Third World conflicts.

Reporter Walter Cronkite (with the microphone) conducting an interview with the commanding officer of the U.S. 1st Marines, 1st Battalion, during the Battle of Hué City, a key moment of the Vietnam War in February of 1968.

In several years of fierce fighting, the Americans and their South Vietnamese allies were unable to achieve a breakthrough. In early 1968 the communist Tet Offensive contradicted U.S. government claims that the war was being won. The credibility of the United States having been undermined rather than enhanced by the war, President Johnson decided it was time to find a way out of Vietnam. This task would fall to his successor, Richard M. Nixon, to carry out.

Unrest, Reform, and Détente

By the late 1960s, activists were also calling for a different policy, and they were able to mobilize a growing number of people. The Vietnam War thus contributed greatly to the rise of yet another global phenomenon—that of the so-called counterculture. Increasingly uncomfortable with the Cold War **status quo**, young people all over the Western world and beyond had begun to protest the war and challenge their leaders on many issues. By the late 1960s, the counterculture—inspired by examples as diverse as Mao's revolutionary writings and the African American movement for civil rights—contributed greatly to social and political turmoil in many Western countries.

Protest against the Vietnam War on October 21, 1967, in Washington, D.C.

Communist governments also had to deal with challenges from within. In China, Mao's "Cultural Revolution"—his campaign against real and potential critics of his regime—threatened to escalate into civil war. In the Soviet Bloc, the movement for "communism with a human face" in Czechoslovakia, also known as the "Prague Spring," directly challenged the communist regime. On top of that, in 1969 the armies of communisms' two greatest powers—the Soviet Union and China—actually fought several skirmishes along their shared border. Finally, the Soviet Union was at last catching up with the United States in the number of intercontinental missiles capable of delivering nuclear warheads to each other's shores. With this came the realization on both sides that war and/or bankruptcy might be right around the corner: it was time that they try to avoid both outcomes.

One way for the governments of the great powers to deal with these challenges was through internal measures. For example, in August 1968, Moscow and its Warsaw Pact allies invaded Czechoslovakia to suppress the reform movement. Another method, however, was a new approach to the Cold War called détente, meaning

A contemporary street scene in Prague (on the left) showing a poster illustrating the 1968 Soviet invasion of the city.

the relaxation of tensions between the two sides. Through détente, the Cold War opponents began to de-emphasize ideological differences and focus on mutually beneficial agreements that would also make conflict less dangerous. While the United States played a central part, it was actually West Germany that took the lead.

Under Chancellor Willy Brandt, the West German government approached the Soviet Union, East Germany, and other Soviet Bloc countries in 1969 to normalize relations frozen by the Cold War. Brandt did not accept the permanent division of Europe and Germany. However, he argued, in order to start chipping away at walls and iron curtains and improve the lives of the people affected by them, the dividing lines first had to be accepted as realities. Within several years, West Germany's new Eastern policy, Ostpolitik, led to a continent-wide détente, culminating in 1975 in the Helsinki conference. There, the countries of Europe, joined by the United States and Canada, agreed that the political status quo could only be changed through peaceful means. There would also be increased economic contacts. Finally, East and West endorsed fundamental human rights as valid for everyone.

At the time, Western governments were criticized for accepting Soviet dominance of Eastern Europe. In the long run, the human rights clauses became a major nuisance for Moscow and its allies, while the legitimacy of their rule remained as shaky as ever. Dissidents and human rights advocates in the West made sure the rights issue remained on the political agenda, and Western governments often followed suit. In this way, the issue of human rights—yet another "global norm" making headway in the 1970s—contributed to the end of the Cold War in the late 1980s.

In the chess game between the great powers—the United States, the Soviet Union, and China—détente also produced significant changes in the 1970s. Seeking their help in finding a way out of Vietnam, but also taking advantage of their feud, the Nixon administration succeeded in improving relations with both communist great powers between 1969 and 1973. With the Soviet Union, Washington entered into talks on a Strategic Arms Limitation Treaty (SALT), something both powers saw as in their interest. The United States also offered Moscow the prospect of greater economic cooperation. In return, it wanted the Soviet leadership's assistance in winding down the Vietnam War. Nixon wanted an outcome that would preserve the South Vietnamese state for at least a few years, a condition often referred to as "peace with honor."

As it conducted these negotiations with the Soviets, the Nixon administration also moved to normalize relations with Communist China. Since Mao's revolution in 1949, Washington had refused to recognize the communist government, and for his part Mao had branded the United States as China's main enemy. Washington now hoped to shore up its international position eroded by Vietnam and the growth of Soviet power. For its part, Beijing was looking for a counterweight against the Soviet menace to Chinese security. Again planning to use the prospect of economic cooperation and access to Western technology, the Nixon administration also tried to enlist China's help in finding an "honorable" way out of Vietnam.

THE RISE OF HUMAN RIGHTS

In 1948, the UN General Assembly adopted the Universal Declaration of Human Rights. The declaration, written against the background of the horrors of World War II, formulated basic rights revolving around freedom and equality and declared that every human being was entitled to them.

Enforcement was a different matter: most nations, both newly formed and existing, guarded their national sovereignty and resisted reforms by other countries or international organizations. In the course of the 1960s, however, NGOs such as Amnesty International, founded in 1961, put the issue on the political agenda through the mobilization of hundreds of thousands of people, primarily in Western countries. Governments had to pay attention, and Western officials began to raise human rights issues in their dealings with left- and right-wing dictatorships, albeit imperfectly.

U.S. president Richard Nixon meeting China's leader Mao Zedong in February 1972 in Beijing. The trip was a major step in the restoration of diplomatic relations with the People's Republic of China, which occurred in 1979.

The End of Détente

In the end, results from great-power détente were mixed. The SALT treaty of 1972 did place limits on United States and Soviet nuclear arsenals, but under the treaty these could continue to grow in size. And while diplomatic ties between the Soviet Union and the United States were more open, the remainder of the decade showed that the fundamental competition between the two systems could not be curbed.

The struggle for influence—especially in the Third World—continued with few restraints, and increasingly the United States saw itself on the defensive. Also, neither Moscow nor Beijing was very helpful in Vietnam. The United States achieved a peace treaty with the North Vietnamese in early 1973 that more or less preserved an independent South Vietnam. However, just two years after the American exit, North Vietnam, still a Soviet ally, overran the South. At that time, communists also came to power in neighboring Laos and Cambodia. In subsequent years, with the United States reeling from its defeat in Southeast Asia, the Soviet Union, together with its Cuban ally, became more active in Africa. When the Soviet Union invaded neighboring Afghanistan in late 1979, Washington officially declared détente over.

Mujahideen—Afghan forces fighting against the Soviet invasion—captured by Soviet forces in 1987.

Chinese leader Deng Xiaoping and U.S. president Jimmy Carter at a welcoming ceremony at the White House in Washington, D.C., in January 1979, as relations between the two countries continued to warm.

In the meantime, however, U.S.–Chinese détente had resulted in the establishment of formal diplomatic relations between the two countries. More important, during the 1970s, the Chinese leadership decided to abandon its militant anti-Western policies. Having reached a dead end under Mao, the revolutionary approach to China's development also was gradually replaced by an evolutionary one. Mao's successor, Deng Xiaoping, aligned foreign and domestic policy after 1976 to promote China's modernization in collaboration with the West. By the end of the decade, China was withdrawing from the Cold War. While politically it remained a communist dictatorship, economically it sought to join the liberal-democratic order—and the emerging global economy, promoted by the United States. In the Third World, Beijing gradually withdrew its support from revolutionary groups and governments.

The significance of these changes only became clear over time. By the late 1970s, the world was entering a new period of East-West confrontation. While Soviet influence seemed to rise, the West experienced a crisis of confidence, to a large extent caused by economic setbacks. In hindsight, we can see the 1970s as a period when the traditional industrial economies of the West began to transform themselves into

King Faisal of Saudi Arabia during a welcoming ceremony at the White House in 1971. Saudi Arabia was one of the leading countries in OPEC, which exercised control over global oil production and prices since its founding in 1960.

the modern service economies of our time. The world also had to get used to higher oil prices set by the Organization of the Petroleum Exporting Countries (OPEC).

The growing influence of OPEC was yet another way in which developed and developing countries became more interdependent, one more sign of globalization. An emerging global division of labor, with industrial production beginning to move from Western countries to so-called emerging economies (for example, in East Asia), also signaled the coming of a new, global economy. In the longer run, the West would be a major beneficiary of globalization. However, during the difficult transition period, things looked glum. This was especially the case for the United States, which in 1979 suffered a major defeat in the Middle East when an Islamist revolution in Iran replaced the Shah, the ally the United States had helped to power in 1953.

In reality, it was the Soviet Union that was falling behind. The invasion of Afghanistan was a rather desperate operation to defend a communist government against local Islamist challengers (the mujahideen), not an expansionist move. When Solidarity, an independent trade union in Poland, threatened the power of the communist government in 1981, Kremlin leaders internally ruled out another intervention. The combined commitments in Eastern Europe, Southeast Asia, Africa, and elsewhere were much more than an increasingly dysfunctional Soviet economy could support. Massive spending on the arms race only made things worse. Unlike the industrial economies of the West, the command economies and closed political system of the Soviet Bloc failed to adjust to the new realities of globalization. By the early 1980s, Moscow was feeling the effects of "imperial overstretch," and an aging, ineffective leadership could do nothing about it.

Because the new chill in East-West relations was real and contacts between the new U.S. government led by Ronald Reagan and the Kremlin were minimal, in 1983 the world experienced another year of crisis. In some ways it was reminiscent of 1962, the year of the Cuban Missile Crisis. Once more, rhetoric and armament policies combined to produce "nuclear fear" among the public. Both sides played their part, but President Reagan's Strategic Defense Initiative (SDI) struck many as unnecessarily provocative. The same went for Reagan's characterization of the Soviet Union as an "Evil Empire."

Once more also, there were small crises that could have developed into larger confrontations, particularly because leaders lacked a good understanding of what motivated the other side. During a NATO exercise in November called Able Archer, for instance, a small war scare developed in Moscow; two months earlier, Soviet jets shot down a South Korean airliner that had strayed into Soviet airspace. Cool heads prevailed during both crises and, as in the 1960s, in the aftermath officials on both sides tried to draw the right lessons.

In 1985 the Soviet Union got a new, young, and ambitious leader in Mikhail Gorbachev. Guided by "new thinking," he and his advisers recognized how the Soviet Union was falling behind in a globalizing world. Gorbachev made it his goal to reform Soviet communism, make it more dynamic, and recommit the population to the system. Beyond general slogans calling for reform (perestroika) and openness (glasnost), his plans remained vague, and in the end Gorbachev failed to give the Soviet system a new lease on life.

Part of Gorbachev's "new thinking" was a redefinition of relations with the West. Here, he was very successful, even though, in the end, better relations with the West could not save the Soviet Union either. Gorbachev, however, was convinced that the nuclear standoff with the West did not serve any useful purpose. In a globalizing world, economics more than nuclear arsenals defined the potential of a country. In his nuclear **abolitionism**, Gorbachev found a partner in President Reagan. Within two years of their first meeting in 1985, the two leaders achieved a breakthrough. From 1987, when the Intermediate Nuclear Forces (INF) Treaty was signed, the arms race was actually put in reverse. The INF Treaty eliminated an entire class of nuclear weapons on both sides, and in later years other agreements reinforced the arms-reduction process.

THE OIL CRISES OF THE 1970S

With economic recovery in the industrialized world after 1945 came dependence on oil, increasingly produced in the Middle East. Production grew fast, and Western oil companies, which maintained the wells, benefited disproportionally, according to the oil-producing countries. These countries, most of them in the Middle East, wanted a bigger share of the proceeds, a goal they pursued via the Organization of the Petroleum Exporting Countries (OPEC), founded in 1960.

In 1971, OPEC negotiated a first increase in the price of oil while also enlarging the share of the proceeds for the producer countries. In 1973, there came another price hike, just before the outbreak of war between Israel and its Arab neighbors. Western support for Israel in that war led to an oil boycott of the West by Middle Eastern countries, which quickly quadrupled the price of oil. It was the beginning of a serious economic slump in the West, prolonged in 1979 when oil prices shot up again after the Islamic Revolution in oil-rich Iran.

Beyond the arms race, Gorbachev began to emphasize that the Soviet Union and the rest of the world had more shared interests than differences. In short, like Deng Xiaoping a decade earlier, Gorbachev began to withdraw his country from the Cold War. The best illustration came in 1989, when the population in the countries that had been in the Soviet Union's European sphere of influence since World War II openly challenged their communist governments. One after the other, these governments lost control. Moscow did nothing to save them. In November, even the Berlin Wall—the symbol of the Cold War division of Europe—was breached by a restless East German population eager for contacts with the West. With that momentous development, the Cold War was officially over, and the world entered a new era.

Former U.S. president Ronald Reagan presents the Reagan Medal of Freedom to former Soviet leader Mikhail Gorbachev in May 1992.

Text-Dependent Questions

1. How was the world becoming more interconnected during the 1960s and 1970s?

2. Define West Germany's Eastern policy, Ostpolitik.

3. What conditions existed in 1979 that might have caused Americans to worry that their country might lose the Cold War after all? What were some of the factors that contributed to the end of the Cold War?

 Research Projects

1. Using Amnesty International's Web site and other materials, write a brief report on the organization, describing its founder, origins, and the methods it uses to place human rights issues on the agendas of politicians and governments.

2. For many people in Eastern Europe, 1989 was the "miracle year" when communism was overthrown peacefully. Starting in 1988, and continuing to the end of 1989, list the major developments in a timeline, and describe in an essay how they may have related to each other.

WORDS TO UNDERSTAND

inflammatory: capable of causing anger and hatred.

intervention: interference in another country's internal affairs or in a conflict between two or more countries.

nepotism: favoritism toward family members in government appointments.

sanctions: measures countries take to punish other countries for behavior deemed unacceptable.

sovereignty: the power states claim to determine their own affairs.

terrorist: relating to violent or destructive acts used to instill fear in a population.

ABOVE: The signing of the agreement that dissolved the Soviet Union into separate republics in December 1991; the breakup was led by Boris Yeltsin (seated second from right), then the leader of Russia, the largest of the republics.

The World Order Challenged, 1990–2015

In 1989 the Cold War ended, although the Soviet Union would exist until the end of 1991. International politics, however, evolved within one single framework: the liberal-democratic order developed after 1945 under U.S. leadership. This did not mean that all nations that participated were democracies. During the 1980s, many developing nations had implemented market reforms. In this, they were often compelled by terms set by the U.S.–dominated International Monetary Fund, to which many of them had turned for financial support. However, political reform often lagged, as was the case in China.

China, Germany, and the Soviet Union

As China opened up its economy to the outside world during the 1980s, aspirations for greater political freedoms began to rise among the population, especially university students. In the spring of 1989, student protests intensified, and they threatened to spread to other parts of the population. Before that could happen, the communist government suppressed the protest movement in a bloody crackdown in Beijing's Tiananmen Square. In the case of China and other countries, participation in the U.S.-led liberal-democratic international system and its institutions would remain conditional.

One immediate challenge after the end of the Cold War was the future of Germany, which was quickly moving toward unification in 1990. The four powers that had occupied the country after World War II (France, Great Britain, the Soviet Union, and the United States), and that had together retained the right to determine the country's future, collaborated with the two German states to guide the process. The new U.S. president, George H. W. Bush, and German chancellor Helmut Kohl also persuaded Soviet leader Gorbachev to agree to NATO membership of the new,

THE MAASTRICHT TREATY

Already before the end of the Cold War, during the 1980s, Western European countries committed to further integration. In a globalizing world, they agreed, the European Economic Community should strive for a single economic market and other forms of cooperation. The end of communism in Eastern and Central Europe and the unification of Germany accelerated the process.

With the Maastricht Treaty of 1992, or Treaty on European Union, member states formally committed themselves to economic and monetary integration, cooperation in law enforcement, and steps toward a common foreign and security policy. The treaty also strengthened the powers of the European parliament. The treaty created the European Union (EU) and EU citizenship for citizens of member countries: from then on, they could move freely in the EU and vote in local elections and in elections for the European parliament.

People join the Toronto Association for Democracy in China in June 2013 to commemorate the bloody crackdown of the Tiananmen Square protest in Beijing in 1989.

unified German state (where the rivaling Warsaw Pact organization dissolved itself in 1991). Kohl also agreed to greater European integration, including the first steps toward a common currency, in return for French support for unification.

The fact that Gorbachev agreed to NATO membership for a united Germany underlined his waning influence, which was evident inside the Soviet Union. Led by the Soviet republics bordering the Baltic Sea, various peoples inside the country now sought independence. Resistance from conservative critics, meanwhile, was growing. In mid-1991, both developments climaxed, signaling the beginning of the end of the Soviet Union. In July, hard-liners in the Soviet leadership staged a coup d'état against Gorbachev. It failed due to the leadership of Boris Yeltsin, the head of the Soviet Union's largest republic, Russia. Yeltsin next moved to force the formal breakup of the country: Russia and all the other Soviet republics were to become independent states by the end of the year, when Gorbachev would formally be out of a job.

Hot Spots and the New World Order

During this time, the focus of world politics had already begun to shift to other regions, particularly the Middle East. In August of 1990, Iraq, led by Saddam Hussein, invaded Kuwait, not only violating a neighboring country's **sovereignty**, but also threatening Saudi Arabia, a vital partner and oil supplier of the West. In his response, President Bush declared the issue a crucial test for what he called the "new world order." The way the world responded would determine the nature of the post–Cold War world, he argued.

Bush proceeded to assemble a U.S.-led coalition, with participation from the Soviet Union and most Arab nations. Sanctioned by a United Nations Security Council resolution, the coalition attacked in early 1991, quickly driving the Iraqis out of Kuwait. Although the road to Baghdad, Iraq's capital, appeared to be open, and Iraqi Shiites and Kurds were ready to assist in overthrowing the Baathist regime, Bush declined to overstep the UN mandate. Saddam was left in power, hopefully reined in by new UN **sanctions**, even though he was a potentially destabilizing force in the region. In the wake of the war, UN inspectors determined that when it invaded Kuwait, Iraq had been two years away from secretly developing a nuclear weapons capability.

The same year, 1991, a new challenge for the "new world order" emerged when the breakup of multinational Yugoslavia—comprising Serbia, Croatia, Slovenia,

Vehicles, both civilian and military, destroyed along the Kuwait City Highway, during the U.S.-led attack against Iraq's invasion of Kuwait in 1989.

THE SREBRENICA MASSACRE OF 1995

The collapse of Yugoslavia after 1990 was especially violent in Bosnia-Herzegovina. There, Bosnian-Serb forces, supported by Serbia proper, sought to take control of most of Bosnia's eastern territory and merge it with Serbia. One of their methods was "ethnic cleansing," or the forcible removal, or murder, of non-Serbs, especially Bosnian Muslims (Bosniaks).

The UN Security Council in 1993 designated several towns as "safe areas" where UN troops would be present to protect local populations. In July 1995, Bosnian-Serb forces went on the attack and overran Srebrenica. France, Britain, and the United States had indicated that no airstrikes or other reinforcements would be provided to Dutch peacekeeping forces in the area. After taking control, Bosnian-Serb forces took 8,000 men and boys from the fenced-off UN "safe area" guarded by the Dutch and murdered them in cold blood. Outrage over the massacre and the failure of the UN mission helped pave the way for the NATO intervention in Bosnia later that year.

RIGHT: Imprisoned for years for his fight against South Africa's apartheid system, Nelson Mandela was instrumental in the country's peaceful transition to democracy. Here, he is celebrated at age 90 on the cover of *Time* magazine.

Bosnia-Herzegovina, Macedonia, and Montenegro—turned violent. Fighting was fierce between Serbian and Croatian forces, but especially between the three major population groups in Bosnia. Several EU and UN diplomatic initiatives failed to stop the conflict, and so-called UN safe areas fell short in practice, most notoriously in Srebrenica in 1995. Eventually, it was U.S.–led **intervention** by NATO and U.S.–led diplomacy, all sanctioned by the UN Security Council, that led to a resolution (the so-called Dayton Accords).

Thus, while the post–Cold War world was far from peaceful, it appeared that the liberal-democratic system led by the United States provided some means with which to pursue peace and stability. The events of the late 1980s and early 1990s also suggested that liberal democracy was a viable model, and this was reinforced by the peaceful dissolution of the racist apartheid system in South Africa. In 1994, Nelson Mandela, the long-imprisoned leader of the African National Congress, was elected president of a country now under a majority-rule system.

Initially, Russia too appeared to be reforming itself along liberal-democratic lines. However, economic challenges remained tremendous. Also, democratization was dealt a heavy blow during a constitutional crisis in 1993, when the Yeltsin government resolved a standoff with parliament through the use of force.

The following year, Moscow also intervened militarily in Chechnya, part of Russia but seeking independence. Among other concerns, especially humanitarian ones, the brutal intervention in Chechnya once again raised questions about the constitutionality of the government's actions. During the Yeltsin era, the country remained a partner of the United States, which invested significant dollars to help secure nuclear equipment and material. At the same time, Russia struggled to find the resources to manage the Soviet Union's nuclear industry. Russia was largely a bystander when, during the 1990s and early 2000s, former members of the Warsaw Pact gained admission to the EU and NATO.

The entry of these formerly communist countries into Western organizations suggested to many people (at least in the West) that free markets, open societies, and the international institutions founded

A man praying in Grozny, the capital of Chechnya, in January 1995 during the Russian army's brutal intervention during the Chechen drive for independence.

since 1945 would define the international system of the twenty-first century. China's efforts to join the World Trade Organization, bearing fruit in 2001, seemed another such sign. Globalization had continued apace after the end of the Cold War, because it appeared to offer the majority of people around the world a view of a better future. Meanwhile, George Bush's "new world order" had been fairly successful during its first decade in providing the framework within which states could make that future a stable and peaceful one. The twenty-first century, it seemed, might well become another "American Century."

Terrorism and the New World Order

The **terrorist** attacks on New York and Washington on September 11, 2001, changed that perspective. The attacks by "al-Qaeda" were a grim reminder that not everyone around the world welcomed the liberal-democratic order. Its leader, Osama bin Laden,

NATO EXPANSION AND RUSSIA

NATO's expansion after the Cold War resulted from choices by Western leaders that at the time seemed both prudent and farsighted.

After the collapse of communism, security in Europe still required U.S. involvement, and the vehicle for it was NATO. Even though Russia was now weak, countries such as Poland, the Czech Republic, and Hungary still hoped to join NATO and also wanted to become part of the EU. The three Central-European states entered the alliance in 1999.

Western governments believed that NATO expansion would contribute to peace and stability. This rationale for NATO membership applied to the newly unified Germany. And after 2000 it would justify the entry of Estonia, Latvia, and Lithuania, all former republics of the Soviet Union. While Russia was never a candidate, in 1997 it did agree to a framework for collaboration called the NATO-Russia Founding Act. Increasingly after 2000, however, Russia came to see NATO as a threat to its interests. In 2015, after the confrontation over Ukraine, NATO-Russia collaboration became impossible.

The South Tower in flames following the deliberate crash of two United Airlines planes into the World Trade Center by al-Qaeda terrorists on September 11, 2001.

had organized al-Qaeda, a radical Islamic terrorist group, in response to the deployment of U.S. troops in Saudi Arabia during the Gulf War of 1991—showing that great-power intervention in the Third World was problematic at least, and **inflammatory** to many, just as it was during the Cold War. What's more, al-Qaeda's ability to train in Afghanistan—a failed state since the Soviet war of the 1980s, if not before—served as a stern reminder that, in a globalizing world, areas left behind could have major disruptive effects far beyond their borders.

The response by the administration of President George W. Bush eventually made things worse. The initial attack on al-Qaeda's staging ground in Afghanistan and the toppling of its Islamist Taliban regime received broad international support. The decision in late 2002 to also attack Saddam Hussein's Iraq to bring about regime change there, however, was extremely controversial. Washington pointed to the danger of Iraq possibly having acquired weapons of mass destruction, but many governments were skeptical. While the Bush administration argued that UN resolutions sanctioned its actions, many other countries, including America's traditional allies France and Germany, did not. That Iraq descended into a bloody insurgency against the American occupiers following the ousting of Hussein, as well as a civil war between the Sunni and Shia factions and the Kurds, did not help.

Bush and his advisers believed an offensive strategy, executed if necessary without formal sanction of the UN Security Council, would be the catalyst of major political change in the Middle East. Once Iraq had a new, representative government, populations in other Arab dictatorships would demand reforms, too, they believed. Political change of that nature, the administration argued, could truly address the root causes of instability and extremism in the region—such as poverty, corrupt governments, ignorance, and religious fundamentalism. Instead, Iraq's bloody chaos provided a new cause, and new opportunities, for Islamic extremist groups. Neighboring Islamist Iran also gained new influence in Iraq and the region at large.

Meanwhile, the fact that the Bush administration did not apply the Geneva Conventions for the treatment of prisoners of war to prisoners captured in what it called the "global war on terror" undermined America's moral authority as the leading power in the international system. Eventually, the American population's war weariness would also complicate the efforts of the country's diplomats to execute international leadership. A further complicating factor was the financial cost of the two wars halfway around the world. When the U.S. and world economy took a nosedive in 2008, America's leadership capabilities were impaired further.

AN ARC OF CRISIS

Political turmoil and violence did not remain confined to Afghanistan and Iraq after 9/11. The years after 2001 revealed many weak states in a region stretching from Nigeria in West-Central Africa, through the Middle East, to Pakistan in South-Central Asia. Legacies of colonial times and Cold War interventions played their part, as did corruption and **nepotism** on the part of local leaders.

America's "war on terror" helped fan the flames, and the popular uprisings of the "Arab Spring" of 2011 further unsettled many countries. Islamic terrorist groups often took advantage, most notoriously the self-named Islamic State (IS) in Syria and Iraq. Refugees from these regions, as well as IS and IS-inspired attacks in Western countries, underline that in our era of globalization, interdependence is indeed a fact of life.

RIGHT: U.S. president George W. Bush speaking at an Army National Guard support facility in Ewing, New Jersey, in 2002, in the midst of his administration's planning for the 2003 invasion of Iraq and the "global war on terror."

The Chinese destroyer *Qingdao* and fuel ship *Hongzehu* arriving in Pearl Harbor, Hawaii, in September 2006; such routine visits represent the growing importance of China's military and its role in shifting the balance of power in the Pacific Ocean.

The events since 2001 all raise the question of whether the international system can function adequately when no power is willing and able to look after its own interests as well as the health of the whole system. This seems particularly pertinent given the fact that the United States has been instrumental in the creation of the system after 1945 and has often acted as its organizing power.

As was the case before 2001, most countries still have a stake in working within, and therefore preserving, the liberal-democratic international order of the post-1945 era, despite all its problems. It remains difficult to see how peace, stability, and prosperity can be better pursued in a globalized world. However, with the diminished ability of the United States to perform its traditional role, a rising and gradually more assertive China, Europe preoccupied primarily with its internal problems, Russia more and more willing to subvert the system, and a crisis area extending from Nigeria on the Atlantic to Pakistan in South-Central Asia, the world's challenges are much greater than they seemed only two decades ago.

The Syrian civil war, begun as part of the "Arab Spring,"
spread to Aleppo, one of the country's oldest cities, in 2012;
seen here is the effect of three car bombs on the city's
central Saadallah al-Jabiri Square, that year.

Text-Dependent Questions

1. Describe the events of 1991 in the Soviet Union and what they led up to.

2. What was the role of the Bosnian-Serb forces in the Srebrenica Massacre of 1995?

3. What were some of the causes of the attacks of September 11, 2001?

Research Projects

1. Chart on a timeline the expansion of NATO after the Cold War, beginning with the agreement on NATO membership for a united Germany. Pay particular attention to what the response of Russia has been at various points in time (1990; during the 1990s; after 2001).

2. List the most important disputes between China and its neighbors to the east over islands and groups of islands in the South China and East China Seas. Using the U.S. State Department Web site (http://www.state.gov/), also discuss why the United States plays a vital role in most of these disputes.

3. Using this volume as a starting point, draw up a chart depicting what has been called here "the international system" of institutions and nations. (You may also include NGOs, such as Amnesty International and Greenpeace, as well as multinational corporations.) Find a way to show the relative significance of the various parts, so that a viewer gets a sense of how the "system" works in practice.

Timeline

1941	*Life* magazine publisher Henry R. Luce coins the term "The American Century" in an article of the same title.
	British prime minister Winston Churchill and U.S. president Franklin D. Roosevelt issue the Atlantic Charter, a set of principles envisioning a liberal-democratic postwar world.
1944	Soviet leader Joseph Stalin agrees to let the Soviet Union join the new United Nations organization.
	The Bretton Woods Conference develops postwar economic institutions geared toward global stability.
1945	World War II comes to an end with the United States dropping two atomic bombs on Japan.
	The United Nations is established to help maintain security and peace in the postwar world.
1946	In crises over Iran and Turkey, Stalin hopes to exploit weak areas on the Soviet Union's periphery.
	British prime minister Churchill speaks of an "Iron Curtain" separating the democratic part of Europe (in the west) from the communist part (in the east).
1947	U.S. president Harry S. Truman articulates a foreign policy aiming to "contain" the further advance of communism and Soviet power, which comes to be known as the "Truman Doctrine."
1948	Stalin begins a blockade of the western part of Berlin, which is located in the Soviet zone of occupation but occupied by the Western allies; in response, the Berlin Airlift begins.
	The UN General Assembly adopts the Universal Declaration of Human Rights.
1949	Two separate German states, one allied with the West and the other with the Soviet Union, are established.
	Chinese communist leader Mao Zedong proclaims the founding of the People's Republic of China, confirming the communist victory in China's long civil war over nationalists.
1950	The North Korean invasion of South Korea begins. The United States defends the South; Communist China helps the North; and the Soviet Union supports both its communist allies, China and North Korea.
	President Truman approves the development of a new type of nuclear weapon, the hydrogen bomb, putting the nuclear arms race in a higher gear.

The United States begins to support the French war effort in Indochina, including Vietnam, against the communist leader Ho Chi Minh.

1952 European Coal and Steel Community (ECSC) is established.

1953 U.S. president Eisenhower directs the Central Intelligence Agency (CIA) to help overthrow the Mossadegh government in Iran.

1954 U.S. president Eisenhower directs the Central Intelligence Agency (CIA) to help overthrow the Arbenz government in Guatemala.

Ho Chi Minh's forces defeat the French in Indochina, and the Eisenhower administration steps in to prevent Ho's communist government from taking over all of Vietnam.

1955 West Germany gains membership in the North Atlantic Treaty Organization (NATO), an alliance of the United States, Great Britain, and other former European allies in World War II.

The Warsaw Pact Treaty Organization is founded as Moscow's answer to NATO.

Developing countries gather in Bandung, Indonesia, to assert their independence from the Cold War rivalries.

1956 Nikita Khrushchev emerges as the new leader in the Soviet Union following Stalin's death in 1953.

The Soviet Union intervenes militarily in Hungary to defend communist power during an uprising there.

1957 The ECSC forms the basis for the European Economic Community, which will eventually lead to the European Union.

The Soviet Union launches Sputnik, the first satellite to be put into orbit.

1959 Fidel Castro leads an anti-American revolution on the island of Cuba.

1960 The Organization of the Petroleum Exporting Countries (OPEC) is founded.

1961 The building of a wall between East and West Berlin separates the communist part of the city (in the east) from the western part.

The Soviets put the first human being into orbit and return him safely to earth.

The initiative begun with the conference in Bandung leads to the founding of the Non-Aligned Movement.

Amnesty International is founded; it is one of several NGOs that will put human rights on the international political agenda.

Timeline (continued)

1962	Nuclear missile sites constructed by the Soviets in Cuba— within close range of the United States—lead to what is referred to as the Cuban Missile Crisis.
1963	The United States and Soviet Union establish a direct telephone connection for future crisis management.
1964	The "Group of 77" is established to unify developing countries within the United Nations; the United Nations Conference on Trade and Development (UNCTAD) first meets, with a similar agenda.
	U.S. president Lyndon B. Johnson escalates the United States' involvement in the Vietnam conflict, fighting on behalf of South Vietnam against the communist North.
1968	Negotiations for the Nuclear Non-Proliferation Treaty are completed; by the mid-1970s, the great majority of the countries of the world have signed on to it.
	Moscow and its Warsaw Pact allies invade Czechoslovakia to suppress the reform movement known as the "Prague Spring."
1969	The Biafra crisis, involving the Nigerian civil war and the famine it produces, becomes one of the first humanitarian crises gaining worldwide publicity thanks to the relatively new technology of television.
	The armies of communism's two greatest powers—the Soviet Union and China—fight several skirmishes along their shared border.
1971	OPEC negotiates a first increase in the price of oil while also enlarging the share of the proceeds for the producer countries.
1972	The SALT treaty is finalized in a period of growing détente; it puts limits on U.S. and Soviet nuclear arsenals, even though, under the treaty, these could continue to grow in size.
1973	The United States achieves a peace treaty with the North Vietnamese that aims to preserve an independent South Vietnam.
	OPEC engineers another oil price hike, just before the outbreak of war between Israel and its Arab neighbors.
1975	The Helsinki conference takes place, where the countries of Europe, with the United States and Canada, agree that peaceful means should be used to decrease the tensions of the Cold War in Europe.
	North Vietnam, still a Soviet ally, overruns South Vietnam, despite the 1973 peace treaty with the United States.

1976	Mao's successor, Deng Xiaoping, promotes China's modernization in collaboration with the West; by the end of the decade, Communist China is withdrawing from the Cold War.
1979	The Soviet Union invades neighboring Afghanistan, and the period of détente with the United States is over.
	An Islamist revolution in Iran deposes the Shah, and the new revolutionary forces storm the U.S. embassy, taking virtually all the employees hostage.
1981	Solidarity, an independent trade union in Poland, threatens the power of the communist, Soviet-backed government, but the Soviet Union doesn't intervene.
1983	U.S. president Ronald Reagan announces his plan for the Strategic Defense Initiative (SDI) and proclaims the Soviet Union an "Evil Empire," intensifying Cold War tensions.
1985	A new, young, and ambitious leader, Mikhail Gorbachev, takes the helm in the Soviet Union.
1987	Gorbachev and Reagan achieve a breakthrough in relations between the Soviet Union and the United States, when the Intermediate Nuclear Forces (INF) Treaty is signed, reversing the arms race.
1989	The Berlin Wall collapses, allowing free movement between East and West Berlin and signaling the end of the Cold War.
	Student-led protests in Tiananmen Square in Beijing, China, are violently suppressed.
1990– 1991	Iraq, led by Saddam Hussein, invades Kuwait, violating a neighboring country's sovereignty; the United States and allies respond militarily, driving the Iraqis out.
1991	The Soviet-led Warsaw Pact dissolves; Gorbachev agrees to NATO membership of the new unified Germany.
	The Soviet Union dissolves into separate republics, a breakup led by Boris Yeltsin, the leader of Russia, the largest of the Soviet republics.
	The breakup of Yugoslavia turns violent, leading to a long civil war between Serbian and Croatian forces, especially among the three major population groups in Bosnia.
1992	The Maastricht Treaty, or Treaty on European Union, goes into effect; member states formally commit themselves to economic and monetary integration.

Timeline (continued)

1993	The Yeltsin government in Russia resolves a standoff with parliament through the use of force.
1994	Russia intervenes militarily in Chechnya, part of Russia but seeking independence.
	Nelson Mandela, South Africa's anti-apartheid leader, is elected president of the country, now under a majority-rule system.
1995	In the civil war in the former Yugoslavia, Bosnian-Serb forces overrun Srebrenica, where they massacre some 8,000 non-Serbians, particularly Bosnian Muslims.
1999	Poland, the Czech Republic, and Hungary, formerly under the Soviet Union's sway, join NATO.
2000	Estonia, Latvia, and Lithuania, all former republics of the Soviet Union, join NATO.
2001	Al-Qaeda, a radical Islamic terrorist group, commits terrorist attacks in New York City and Washington, D.C., which will eventually launch a U.S.–led "war on terror."
2003	Under U.S. president George W. Bush, the United States attacks Iraq, dismantling Saddam Hussein's government, but leaving chaos in its wake.
2011	Revolt in Tunisia against the ruling elites there begins the "Arab Spring," in which several countries in the Middle East undergo popular uprisings; unrest in Syria against the Assad regime begins.
2012	Fighting in Syria spreads to its capital, Damascus, and Aleppo, major population centers in the country; the UN declares the conflict to be a civil war.
2014	Conflict in the Ukraine leads to the Russian takeover of the Crimea and continues through to 2015 and beyond; NATO–Russia collaboration becomes impossible.
2016	Terrorist attacks in Paris, Beirut, San Bernardino, and Jakarta (Indonesia) increase concerns over instability in South Asia and the Middle East, including the "Islamic State," which takes advantage of the region's volatility.

Further Research

BOOKS

Fasula, Linda. *An Insider's Guide to the UN*. 3rd ed. New Haven, CT: Yale University Press, 2015.

Kalaitzidis, Akis, and Gregory W. Streich. *U.S. Foreign Policy: A Documentary and Reference Guide*. Santa Monica, CA: Greenwood, 2011.

Shepard, Todd. *Voices of Decolonization: A Brief History with Documents*. New York: Bedford/St. Martin's, 2015.

Steger, Manfred. *Globalization: A Very Short Introduction*. 3rd ed. New York: Oxford University Press, 2013.

Van Dijk, Ruud, ed. *Encyclopedia of the Cold War*. New York: Routledge, 2008.

ONLINE

Arms Control Association: "The Nuclear Nonproliferation Treaty: History and Current Problems": https://www.armscontrol.org/act/2003_12/Bunn.

Cold War International History Project: https://www.wilsoncenter.org/program/cold-war-international-history-project.

Council on Foreign Relations: U.S.–Russia Arms Control: 1949 to the Present" [interactive timeline]: http://www.cfr.org/nonproliferation-arms-control-and-disarmament/us-russia-arms-control/p21620.

John F. Kennedy Presidential Library and Museum: "The Cold War": http://www.jfklibrary.org/JFK/JFK-in-History/The-Cold-War.aspx.

The National Security Archive: http://nsarchive.gwu.edu.

United Nations Archives and Records Management Section: https://archives.un.org/.

NOTE TO EDUCATORS: This book contains both imperial and metric measurements as well as references to global practices and trends in an effort to encourage the student to gain a worldly perspective. We, as publishers, feel it's our role to give young adults the tools they need to thrive in a global society.

Index

Italicized page numbers refer to illustrations

A

Adenauer, Konrad 21
Afghanistan 38, *38,* 40, 50–51
Africa 32–33, 48, *48,* 51
African National Congress 48
al-Qaeda 49, *50*
"American Century, The" (Luce) 9–10
Amnesty International 37
apartheid system 48, *48*
Arab Spring (2011) 51, *52*
Arbenz, Jacobo 25
arms race 13, 19–20, 25–28, *27, 30*
Asia 9–10, 12–13, 18–21, 32–33, 40–41, 51–52. *See also* Vietnam War
Atlantic Charter 10
atomic energy and weapons *12,* 12–13, 19, 24–26, 31

B

Bandung Conference (1955) 32–33
Berlin and Berlin Wall 17–18, *18,* 22, *23,* 42
Biafra, Independent Republic of 33
bin Laden, Osama 49–50
Bosnia-Herzegovina 48
Bosnian civil war 48
Brandt, Willy 36
Bretton Woods Conference (1944) 11
Britain 10, 12–13, 17–18, 20, 27–28, 32–33, 45
Bush, George H. W. 45
Bush, George W. 47, 49–51, *51*

C

Cambodia 38
Canada 18, 36
capitalism 11–13, 18
Carter, Jimmy *39*
Castro, Fidel 26
Chechnya 49, *49*
Checkpoint Charlie *23. See also* Berlin Wall
China 19–21, 24–26, 33–35, *37, 39,* 45, *46,* 52, *52*
Churchill, Winston 10, *11,* 13
CIA (Central Intelligence Agency) *24,* 25–26
Cold War: and arms race 28, *30*; and globalization 31–33; political ideology 12–13, 42; and Third World 20, 33; U.S. role in 9, 13–14, 26
colonialism 10, 17, 19–21, 25, 32–33. *See also* Third World countries
communism 11–14, 18, *19,* 24–26, 34–35, 41, 45–46, 50
Communist New Fourth Army (China) *19*
containment policy 13–14, 18, 20. *See also* Cold War
Cronkite, Walter *34*
Cuba 26–27, *28,* 38, 41
Cuban Missile Crisis (1962) 26, *28,* 41
Czechoslovakia and Czech Republic 18, 35, *36,* 50

D

Dayton Accords (1995) 48
Deng Xiaoping 39, *39,* 42
détente 35–39
developing nations 19, 32–33, 40, 45. *See also* Third World countries

E

Eastern Europe 12, 22, 35–37, 40, 42, 46, 49. *See also* Europe
East Germany (German Democratic Republic) 22, 36, 42. *See also* Germany
economic recession (2008) 51
Eisenhower, Dwight D. *24,* 25
Estonia 50
ethnic cleansing 48
Europe: colonial empires 10, 19–20, 25, 32; integration of 21, *22,* 46, 49–50; Soviet influence in 18, 22, 24, 33, 36, 40–42, 50; World War II and postwar economic recovery 9–10, 13–14, *16,* 17, 21, *22,* 46
European Coal and Steel Community (ECSC) 21, *22*
European Economic Community 21, *22,* 46
European Union (EU) 21, *22,* 46, 49–50

F

Faisal bin Abdulaziz (king, Saudi Arabia) *40*
France 17–20, 45, 48
free trade 10, 49
French Communist Congress (1921) 21

G

Geneva Conventions 51
Germany: division and Soviet influence 12–13, *17–18,* 32, 36; economic recovery 18, 21; NATO membership 50–51; unification 45–46; World

War II defeat *8,* 9–10, *14*
globalization 9, 31–33, 40, 49, 51
Global South and North 19–20, 32–33. *See also*
  Third World
Gorbachev, Mikhail 41–42, *42,* 45–46
Great Britain. *See* Britain
Greece 13–14, *14*
Greek People's Liberation Army (ELAS) *14*
Group of 77 (United Nations) 33
Guatemala 25
Gulf War (1991) 47, *47,* 50–51, *51*

H

Helsinki Accords (1975) 36
Hiroshima 12–13
Hitler, Adolf *8,* 9–10
Ho Chi Minh (Nguyen Ai Quoc) 21, *21,* 25
human rights 36–37
Hungary 22, 50
hydrogen bomb *20,* 26, *27. See also* nuclear
  weapons

I

IMF (International Monetary Fund) 11, 45
imperialism 14
India 20, *32*
Indochina 20–21, 25, *34,* 34–35, *35,* 37–38
Indonesia 20–21, *32*
Intermediate Nuclear Forces Treaty (1987) 41
International Atomic Energy Agency 31
Iran 13, *24,* 25, 40–41
Iraq 47, *47,* 50–51, *51*
Iron Curtain 13
ISIS (Islamic State of Iraq and Syria) 51. *See also*
  terrorism
isolationism 9
Israel *32,* 41
Italy *14, 16*

J

Japan 9–10, 12–13, 18–19, 32
Johnson, Lyndon B. 34–35

K

Kennan, George F. 13–14
Kennedy, John F. *23,* 26–27
Khrushchev, Nikita 22, 26–27
Kohl, Helmut 45–46
Korea 20, *32*
Kurds 47, 51
Kuwait 47, *47*

L

Laos 38
Latvia 50
liberal-democratic international order 10–11,
  14, 21, 39, 45, 48–49, 52
Lithuania 50
Luce, Henry R. 9–10, *10*

M

Maastricht Treaty (Treaty on European Union,
  1992) 46
Macedonia 48
Mandela, Nelson 48, *48*
Mao Zedong 19, 21, 26, 35, *37,* 39
market economy 11, 14, 45
Marshall Plan 14, *16*
Middle East 13, 32–33, 41, 47, 51, *52*
Montenegro 48
Mossadegh, Mohammed *24,* 25
Mujahideen *38,* 40
Muslims 48
Mussolini, Benito *8*

N

Nagasaki 12–13
nationalist governments 19, *19,* 25
NATO North Atlantic Treaty Organization 18,
  21, 45–46, 48–50
NATO-Russia Founding Act (1997) 50
Nazis *8, 14*
Nehru, Jawaharlal 20
Netherlands 20
new world order 47–49
Nigeria 33, 51
Nixon, Richard M. 35, *37*
Non-Aligned Movement *32,* 32–33. *See also*
  Third World
non-governmental organizations (NGOs) 33, 37
North Korea 20, *32*
Nuclear Non-Proliferation Treaty (1968) 31, *32*
nuclear weapons: arms race 13, 25–28, *28,*
  30–31; nonproliferation 28, *32,* 33, *37*–38,
  41; and Soviet Union 13, 31, 35, 49; and
  Third World nations *32,* 47; and United
  States 20, *27, 30*

O

oil production 40, *40,* 41
OPEC (Organization of the Petroleum Export-
  ing Countries) 40, *40,* 41
Ostpolitik 36

Index (continued)

P

Pakistan 20, *32*, 51
Partial Test Ban Treaty (1963) 28
People's Republic of China 19, *37. See also China*
Poland 12, *17*, 40, 50
Potsdam Conference (1945) *12*
Prague Spring 35, *36. See also* Czechoslovakia

R

Reagan, Ronald 40–42, *42*
religion 40–41, 47–48, 51
Roosevelt, Franklin D. 9–10, *11*
Russia *17*, 46, *49*, 52. *See also* Soviet Union

S

Saddam Hussein 47, 50–51
Saudi Arabia *40*, 47, 50
Schuman, Robert 21
September 11, 2001 attacks 49, *50. See also* terrorism
Serbia 47–48
service economies 40
Shiites 47, 51
Sino-Soviet split 33–35
Six Day War (1967) 41
Slovenia 47–48
Solidarity trade union (Poland) 40
South Africa 48, *48*
South Korea 20. *See also* Korea
Soviet bloc 12, 22, 35–37, 40, 42, 46, 49
Soviet Union: détente and Sino-Soviet split 33–36; invasion of Afghanistan 30, 38, *38*; postwar economic policy 11–12, 14, 18, 22, 40, 45; reforms and dissolution of 41, *44*, 46; and space and arms race 13, 19, 25–28; and Third World countries 26, 38
Srebrenica massacre (1995) 48
Stalin, Joseph *11*, 11–12, *12*, 22
Strategic Arms Limitation Treaty (SALT) 37–38
Strategic Defense Initiative (SDI) 41
Sukarno 20, *32*
Sunnis 51
Syrian civil war *52*

T

Taliban regime 50. *See also* Afghanistan
technology 31–33, 37
terrorism 49–51, *50*, 51, *51*
Third World countries 17, 19–21, 25–26, 32–33, 38–39, 50
Truman, Harry S. 12, *12*, 13–14, *24*
Truman Doctrine 13–14
Turkey 13–14
two camps theory 14

U

Ukraine 50
United Nations 11, 20, 33, 37, 47–48, 51
United Nations Conference on Trade and Development (UNCTAD) 33
United Nations Monetary and Financial Conference (Bretton Woods, 1944) 11
United States: and arms race 13, 25–28, *27, 30*; and China relations 37, *37*, 39, *39*; containment policy 13–14; Cuban Missile Crisis (1962) 26, *28*, 41; Gulf War (1991) 47, *47, 50–51, 51*; and liberal-democratic international order 10–11, 14, 21, 39, 45, 48–49, 52; postwar leadership and economic policy 9–11, 18, 24, 32; role in Europe 17–18, 36, 45; and terrorism 51, *51*; and Third World nations 24–25, 38; Vietnam War 20–21, 25, *34*, 34–35, *35*, 37–38
Universal Declaration of Human Rights 37

V

Vietnam War 20–21, 25, *34*, 34–35, *35*, 37–38

W

Warsaw Pact Treaty Organization 22, 35, 46, 49
weapons of mass destruction 50–51. *See also* Gulf War (1991)
West Germany 17–18, 21–22, 36. *See also* Germany
World Trade Center *50. See also terrorism*
World Trade Organization 49
World War II *8*, 9–11, *14, 17*, 19, 22, 37, 42, 45

Y

Yeltsin, Boris *44*, 46, 48–49
Yugoslavia 47–48

Photo Credits

Page number	Page location	Archive/Photographer
8	Top	Shutterstock/Everett Historical
10	Bottom	Wikimedia Commons /Library of Congress
11	Top	Wikimedia Commons/National Archives and Records Administration
12	Bottom	Wikimedia Commons/National Archives and Records Administration
14	Top	Wikimedia Commons / Greek Diplomatic and Historical Archive Department
16	Top	Wikimedia Commons/National Archives and Records Administration
17	Bottom	Original map based on Wikimedia Sources
18	Bottom	Wikimedia Commons/ /U. S. Department of Agriculture
19	Top	Shutterstock/Everett Historical
21	Top	Wikimedia Commons /Agence de presse Meurisse
22	Bottom	Wikimedia Commons /Glentamara
23	Full page	Wikimedia Commons /Robert Knudsen, White House
24	Top	Wikimedia Commons /Nara.gov
27	Top	Wikimedia Commons
28	Bottom	Wikimedia Commons /CIA
30	Top	Wikimedia Commons
32	Top	Wikimedia Commons
32	Bottom	Wikimedia Commons /Onbekend
34	Bottom	Wikimedia Commons/National Archives and Records Administration
35	Middle	Wikimedia Commons /Frank Wolfe
36	Top	Wikimedia Commons /Adam Jones, Ph.D.
37	Bottom	Wikimedia Commons/National Archives and Records Administration
38	Bottom	Wikimedia Commons/Кувакин Е.
39	Top	Wikimedia Commons/National Archives and Records Administration
40	Top	Wikimedia Commons/Robert L. Knudsen
42	Bottom	Wikimedia Commons/Ronald Reagan Library
44	Top	Wikimedia Commons/U. Ivanov
46	Top	iStock/Canadapanda
47	Bottom	Wikimedia Commons/Capt. R.J. Worsley
48	Bottom	Shutterstock/Popartic
49	Top	Wikimedia Commons/Михаил Евстафьев
50	Top	Wikimedia Commons/Robert J. Fisch
51	Bottom	iStock/EdStock
52	Top	Wikimedia Commons/ Chief Mass Communication Specialist Joe Kane, USN
52	Bottom	Wikimedia Commons/Zyzzzzzy
Cover	Top	Library of Congress
Cover	Left	iStock/vichinterlang
Cover	Right	Shutterstock/Prederic Legrand - COMEO

About the Author and Advisor

Series Author and Advisor

Ruud van Dijk teaches the history of international relations at the University of Amsterdam, the Netherlands. He studied history at Amsterdam, the University of Kansas, and Ohio University, where he obtained his Ph.D. in 1999. He has also taught at Carnegie Mellon University, Dickinson College, and the University of Wisconsin-Milwaukee, where he also served as editor at the Center for 21st Century Studies. He has published on the East-West conflict over Germany during the Cold War, the controversies over nuclear weapons in the 1970s and 1980s, and on the history of globalization. He is the senior editor of the *Encyclopedia of the Cold War* (2008) produced with MTM Publishing and published by Routledge.